These Branching Moments

THESE
BRANCHING
MOMENTS

Forty Odes by

RUMI

Translated by
John Moyne & Coleman Barks

Copper Beech Press

Some of these translations originally appeared in *Plainsong.*

Cover: "Rumi Handing Out Sweets," 17th or 18th century Turkish miniature. Copyright © 1987 by The Museum of Fine Arts, Boston.

The publication of this book was supported in part by a grant from the Boyd Research Center, University of Georgia.

For information, address the publisher:
Copper Beech Press
English Department
Box 1852
Brown University
Providence, Rhode Island 02912

Library of Congress Cataloging in Publication Data
Jalāl al-Dīn Rūmī, Maulana, 1207-1273.
  These branching moments.

  I. Barks, Coleman. II. Title.
PK6480.E5B37   1987   895'.5511   87-36429
ISBN 0-914278-50-9 (pbk.)

First Edition
Printed in the United States of America

for Robert Bly

Introduction

Jelaluddin Rumi was born on the far eastern edge of the Persian empire in Balkh (Afghanistan) on September 30, 1207. His father, Bahauddin Veled, was a famous teacher from a long line of teachers, scholars, theologians, and jurists. When Rumi was still a child, the entire family was exiled from Balkh by the approach of Genghis Khan's armies. After some years of traveling they settled in Konya (Turkey), the western terminus of the Silk Road in the 13th century and thus the melding place of many cultures —Islamic, Judeo-Christian, Hindu, and Buddhist. Rumi's father became the head of a *medrese* (dervish learning community), and Rumi succeeded him in this position. Rumi married and had two sons, Sultan Veled and Allaudin, by his first wife, who died young, and two more children in his second marriage.

Rumi's fairly predictable life changed completely when, at thirty-seven, he met the mysterious Shams of Tabriz. Little is known, for certain, of Shams. He was a wandering dervish, probably about sixty. He had searched the Near East his entire life for someone of great spiritual attainment, a Friend of the Heart. He claimed the *gnosis* of a deep communion that he had never found with a living teacher: "Everyone talks about themselves and their own sheikh as if they thus formed a tie between themselves and truth. But the Prophet of God himself placed the cloak on my shoulders in the spiritual world. This cloak is not one that wears thin in two days, which tears and rots and is thrown away. . . .This cloak is that of *sohbet* and truth. . . .It has no yesterday, nor today, nor tomorrow. . . .What has love to do with time and place?" The word *sohbet* has no English equivalent; it means something like "mystical conversation on mystical subjects."

Shams kept fleeing from the students who always gathered around him, for he sought the reality of *sohbet*. He found it when he met Rumi on an afternoon in November of 1244. For three years they were more or less constantly together in this state. Then Shams disappeared, probably murdered by jealous students. But the work of transformation had begun. Rumi became a fountain of the longing and knowing, that state of Union with the Friend that he found with Shams. He produced the enormous *Divani Shamsi Tabriz* ("The Works of Shams of Tabriz," 42,000 lines of poetry) and the *Mathnawi* (six volumes).

For seven centuries much of the Near East and Asia have loved Rumi and translated his poetry into their faiths. It might be said that Rumi did not see the separate streams of different religions, but rather the ocean into which they were pouring. "I go into the Christian church," he said, "and the Jewish synagogue, and the Muslim mosque, and I see only *one* altar."

On the cover of this book, Rumi is distributing little tastes of sweetness. There is that quality in the odes, of a gift that exfoliates into a community of giving. The poems circulate through the tangents of joy and longing, and then dissolve into silence, the deep sky-silence around the words. Rumi often flees back into it at the end of a poem:

> The speechless full moon
> comes out now.

Or:

> No more garlicky detail, no more meanings.
> Only clean-breathed,
> silent escaping.

Sometimes he implies that the silence will keep writing the poem after he stops:

> Those two, [thinking and imagining]
> they are so thirsty, but this gives smoothness
> to water. Their mouths are dry and they are tired.

> The rest of this poem is too blurry
> for them to read.

Beyond "sensory imagination" and "thinking," these poems grow from another broken ground. He didn't write them; he spoke them and his students, or a scribe, took them down. They move quickly, like spirit, yet they carefully love the world-stuff they're made of: the animals, the plants, "the details of any story." They stand still and soar at the same time.

Even Kemal Ataturk, warrior and founder of modern Turkey, the man who forcibly tried to secularize the country, had this to say of Rumi: "Every visitor to Mevlana's Mausoleum is a refugee from reactionary dogma. . .to the idea of soaring to God, standing, whirling. . . .Mevlana is a lover of transformation who transcends the ages."

Rumi's era was, like ours, a time of violent sectarian conflict, with many religions jostling for power and spheres of influence. It was dangerous to be known as a "mystic," but Rumi somehow became a haven of inclusiveness. "The day will come," he once told his son, "when many people will come to Konya to visit our graves and speak our words."

Rumi died at sunset on December 17, 1273. It is said that everybody came to his funeral — Christians, Hindus, and Buddhists. His presence was larger than any doctrine or church; his poetry has always found *lovers* in every tradition. There is today a Christian church in Shiraz (Iran) that has lines from Rumi carved in stone around the door:

> Where Jesus lives, the great-hearted gather.
> We are a door that is never locked.
>
> If you are suffering any kind of pain,
> Stay near this door. Open it.

The anniversary of Rumi's death, called his "Wedding Night," is celebrated in Konya and elsewhere with a *sema*, the majestic "turning" meditation that Rumi originated. When the greatest spiritual poet of this century, Rainer Maria Rilke, saw the Mevlevi dervishes in Cairo on December 17, 1910, he wrote: "It is so truly the mystery of the kneeling of the deeply kneeling man. . .which is celebrated in this night. . . .With him the scale is shifted, for in following the peculiar weight and strength in his knees. . .he. . . belongs to that world in which height is — depth. . . .This is the night of radiant depth unfolded."

Rilke might just as well have been describing the opening that occurs in Rumi's odes. His poetry is surrendered ground, a big mirror laid out in the long grass. His vision sees the Friend or Beloved in every object and every face, in light itself:

> This day is conscious of itself.
> This day is a lover, bread and gentleness.

Coleman Barks

A Note on These Translations

These are collaborative translations. Seven of them (3, 4, 13, 21, 28, 29, 35) were done with John Moyne (Head of Linguistics, City University of New York); the others are the results of my working with the A. J. Arberry texts. In the standard Persian text of Rumi's work *(Kullyat-e Shams,* ed. Furuzanfar, 8 vols., 1957-66), the odes are numbered. For reference, the Furunzanfar numbers of the odes in this book are, in order: 2003, 1139, 255, 3438, 809, 2530, 1472, 3051, 3055, 1807, 3048, 879, 1703, 2405, 2865, 2880, 1380, 2902, 598, 791, 2302, 2135, 636, 310, 2894, 1073, 2779, 1924, 1923, 3034, 1121, 2958, 2728, 2967, 2544, 1628, 2322, 996, 2166, 1538.

C.B.

1

Everyone has eaten and fallen asleep. The house is empty.
We walk out to the garden to let the apple meet the peach,
to carry messages between rose and jasmine.

Spring is Christ,
raising martyred plants from their shrouds.
Their mouths open in gratitude, wanting to be kissed.
The glow of the rose and the tulip means a lamp
is inside. A leaf trembles. I tremble
in the wind-beauty like silk from Turkestan.
The censor fans into flame.

This wind is the Holy Spirit.
The trees are Mary.
Watch how husband and wife play subtle games with their hands.
Cloudy pearls from Aden are thrown across the lovers,
as is the marriage custom.

The scent of Joseph's shirt comes to Jacob.
A red carnelian of Yemeni laughter is heard
by Muhammed in Mecca.

We talk about this and that. There's no rest
except on these branching moments.

2

If a tree could fly off, it wouldn't suffer the saw.
The sun hurries all night to be back for morning.
Salty water rises in the air, so the garden
will be drenched with fresh rain.

A drop leaves home, enters a certain shell, and becomes a pearl.
Joseph turns from his weeping father, toward Egypt.
Remember how that turned out!

Journeys bring power and love
back into you. If you can't go somewhere,
move in the passageways of the self.
They are like shafts of light,
always changing, and you change
when you explore them.

3

Wake up with the morning breeze
and ask for a change. Open and fill yourself
with the wine that is your life.
Pass it around. Pass it to me first!
Revive me with your waking.
Listen to the harp-sound, and sing.
Dawn-music is your joy.
Give me your excitement, but let it ground me,
so I don't wander. Watch the ripples
on the surface. Then launch me
like a ship. Once I was only a piece of wood.
Then Moses threw me down,
and now I'm a powerful dragon. I was dead.
Jesus raised me. Muhammed spoke,
and this tree shimmered.

Say the word again, Shams,
so we can feel you, your light
within everything.

4

Light again, and the One who brings light!
Change the way you live!

From the ocean-vat, wine-fire in each cup!
Two or three of the long dead wake up.
Two or three drunks become lion-hunters.

Sunlight washes a dark face.
The flower of what's true opens in the face.
Meadowgrass and garden ground grow damp again.
A strong light like fingers massages our heads.
No dividing these fingers from those.

Draw back the lock-bolt.
One level flows into another.
Heat seeps into everything.
The passionate pots boil.
Clothing tears into the air.
Poets fume shreds of steam,
never so happy as out in the light!

Steam fills the bath and frozen figures on the wall
open their eyes, wet and round, Narcissus eyes
that see enormous distances. And new ears
that love the details of any story. The figures dance
like friends diving into red wine, coming up and diving again.

Steam spills into the courtyard. It's the noise
of resurrection. They move from one corner
laughing across to the opposite corner. No one notices
how the steam opens the rose of each mind,
fills every beggar's cup solid with coins.
Hold out a basket. It fills up so well
that emptiness becomes what you want.

The judge and the accused forget the sentencing.
Someone stands up to speak, and the wood of the table
becomes holy. The tavern in that second is actually *made*
of wine. The dead drink it in.
                                    Then the steam evaporates.
The figures sink back into the wall, eyes blank,
ears just lines.
                        Now it's happening again, outside.
The garden fills with bird and leaf sounds.

We stand in the wake of this chattering and grow airy.
How can anyone say what happens, even if each of us
dips a pen a hundred million times into ink?

6

I become a pen in the Friend's hand,
tonight writing *say*, tomorrow *ray*.
He trims the pen for fine calligraphy.
The pen says, *I am here, but who am I?*

He blackens the pen's face.
He wipes it in his hair. He holds it upside down.
Now he begins to use it.

On one sheet he cancels everything.
On another he adds a dangerous conjunction.
The writing depends entirely on the scribe,
who knows how to split the head of the pen.

Galen knows what a patient needs.
The pen cannot speak for itself, or know what
to disapprove of in its own nature.

Whether I say *pen* or *flag*, it is with this wonderful
conscious unconsciousness: the mind unable to include
its own description, composing blindly.
Held in a hand, yet free.

7

I have broken out again,
escaped from the tricky,
wiry shamans of ecstasy.

Running night and day to escape night and day.
Why fear grief
when Death walks so close beside?

Don't fear the General
if you're good friends with the Prince.

For forty years I made plans and worried about them.
Now sixty-two, I've escaped reasonableness.

By definition, human beings do not see or hear.
I broke loose from definition.

Skin outside, seeds inside,
a fig lives caught between, and like that fig,
I wriggle free.

Hesitation, deadly. Hurrying, worse.
Escape both delay and haste.

Fed first with blood in the womb,
then milk from the breast,
my clever teeth came in,
and I escaped even those.

Off balance, I grope for bread, a loaf or two,
until God gives the next food,
and I'm gone.

No more garlicky detail, no more meanings.
Only clean-breathed,
silent escaping.

8

How did you get away?
You were the pet falcon of an old woman.
Did you hear the falcon-drum?
You were a drunken songbird put in with owls.
Did you smell the odor of a garden?
You got tired of sour fermenting
and left the tavern.

You went like an arrow to the target
from the bow of time and place.
The man who stays at the cemetery pointed the way,
but you didn't go.
You became light and gave up wanting to be famous.
You don't worry about what you're going to eat,
so why buy an engraved belt?

I've heard of living at the center, but what about
leaving the center of the center?
Flying toward thankfulness, you become
the rare bird with one wing made of fear,
and one of hope. In autumn,
a rose crawling along the ground in the cold wind.
Rain on the roof runs down and out by the spout
as fast as it can.

Talking is pain. Lie down and rest,
now that you've found a friend to be with.

9

You won't find another friend like me.
You spend your days in all directions.
No one accepts your money but me.
You're the dry ditch, and I am rain.
You're the rubble of a building.
I'm the architect.

There is only one sunrise a day.
In your sleep you see many shapes and people.
When you wake, you see nothing.
Close those eyes and open these eyes.

What you've been wanting is a donkey lying sick
on the ground. What you've been doing
is the bit and halter on that donkey.
There's sweet syrup here where you've been buying vinegar
and unripened fruit. Walk into the hospital.
There's no shame in going where everyone has to go.
Without that healing, you're a body
with no head. Be a turban wound around the head.

The mirror is black and rusty.
Who is the lucky man doing business with?
Think of the one who gave you thought.
Walk toward whoever gave you feet.
Look for the one behind your seeing.
Sing and clap because the whole ocean is a bit of foam.
No accidents are happening here.

Listen within your ear. Speak without forming words.
Language turns against itself and is likely
to cause injury.

I've heard enough *dos* — "Dismount" —
when I'm still looking for the road. Enough *gos* —
"Let's go" — before I've even set up my tent.

Could I be spared these *gos* and *dos?*
Will I get to the moonshaped threshing floor
before I die? I feel blessed with this wandering
in the love-sun, but I do not see the road.
I know it's here somewhere,
but I don't see its justice, or its peace.

I ask the wind for word.
I look in wells for the moon's image.
I'm drying up like an August garden.

But I learn quickly
like the same spot in Spring,
in both states amazed at what happens
to just a piece of ground.

11

I feel like the ground, astonished
at what the atmosphere has brought to it. What I know
is growing inside me. Rain makes
every molecule pregnant with a mystery.
We groan with women in labor.
The ground cries out, *I Am Truth* and *Glory Is Here*,
breaks open, and a camel is born out of it.
A branch falls from a tree, and there's a snake.

Muhammed said: *A faithful believer is a good camel,*
always looking to its Master, who takes perfect care.
He brands the flank.
He sets out hay.
He binds the knees with reasonable rules,
and now he loosens all bindings and lets his camel dance,
tearing the bridle and ripping the blankets.

The field itself sprouts new forms,
while the camel dances over them, imaginary
plants no one has thought of,
but all these new seeds, no matter how they try,
do not reveal the other sun.
They hide it.
Still, the effort is joy,
one by one to keep uncovering
pearls in oyster shells.

12

Morning: a polished knifeblade,
the smell of white camphor burning.

The sky tears his blue Sufi robe
deliberately in half.

Daylight Rumi drags his dark opposite
out of sight. A happy Turk comes in.
A grieving Hindu leaves.

The King of the Ethiopians goes.
Caesar arrives.

No one knows how what changes,
changes.

One half of the planet is grass.
The other half grazing.

A pearl goes up for auction. No one has enough,
so the pearl buys itself.

We stand beside Noah and David and Rabia
and Jesus and Muhammed.

Quietness again lifts and planes out,
the blood in our heads gliding
in the sky of the brain.

13

A black sky hates the moon. I am that dark
nothing. I hate those in power.
I'm invited in from the road to the house,
but I invent some excuse.
Now I'm angry at the road.

I don't need love. Let something break me.
I don't want to hear anyone's trouble.
I've had my chance for wealth and position.
I don't want those.

I am iron, resisting the most enormous Magnet there is.
Amber pulls straw to it. That makes me angry.
We're molecules spinning here, four, five, six of us.
What does that mean, *five, six?*
I am angry at God.

You don't understand, being out of the water.
You resemble the sun? I hate likenesses.

14

The sun comes up out of the water.
Dust motes fill with music.
La ilaha illa 'llah.
There is no reality but God.

Why mention flecks of dust?
When the sun of the soul's intelligence arrives,
it wears no cloak and no hat.
Then the moon, the soul's love, rises out of watery hills,
and the sun goes down, Joseph into his well.

Point your head out of the ground like an ant.
Walk onto the threshing floor with new information:
we've been so happy with rotten bits of grain
because we didn't know about these sweet green ears.
It is so simple to say, *We have hands and feet.*
We can walk into the open!

Why mention ants?
Solomon himself tears his robe with wanting this we try to say
with useless imagery.

Language is a tailor's shop where nothing fits.
They've cut and sewn a gown to fit the figure
of the buyer. The gown's too long.
The buyer's too short.

Bring a taller person.
The tape measure is a bowstring as long as from here
to the moon. Bring someone that tall.

Now I'll be quiet and let silence
separate what is true from what are lies
as threshing does.

Be with those who help your being.
Don't sit with indifferent people, whose breath
comes cold out of their mouths.
Not these visible forms, your work is deeper.

A chunk of dirt thrown in the air breaks to pieces.
If you don't try to fly,
and so break yourself apart,
you will be broken open by death,
when it's too late for all you could become.

Leaves get yellow. The tree puts out fresh roots
and makes them green.
Why are you so content with a love that turns you yellow?

With the sacredness you give and describe,
turn us upside down that other people
may know you're here. We're tired of secret joy,
bashfulness and being ashamed.

Reasons for holding back fly off like doves.
You speak your subtle truth to this ring of blank faces,
and someone suddenly finds something in a pile of ashes.

Why am I talking? You know what's happening.
Simply say it.
Walk around to each of us and pour the wine
and spoon out that eggplant fricassee concoction!

Yesterday you put a crown on my head that,
no matter how anyone strikes it,
will not fall off, Love's nightcap,
with your handstitching around the brow.

Even if my head's not in it,
because it is your gift to me,
my head becomes a pearl
lifted from the jewelbox.

Prove it. Here's a heavy mace.
See if I am more bone and marrow
than soul.

Inside this skull-nut there's almond essence
to sweeten lip and throat
and put light in the eyes.

So no more complaining. Jesus didn't ask,
"Where's my donkey?" There was just
one less in the donkey herd.

The strength of a rider doesn't come from his lean mount
but from his love.

Don't say *Ah, ah,* when you're hurt.
Say *Allah.*

Joseph didn't talk about his time down in the well,
but rather of sitting on the throne of Egypt.

You who have done great things, listen to the reed,
the reed, the voice of the reed.
What is the reed? The lover's place to kiss,
place to kiss, the lover's place to kiss.
With no hands and feet, it serves. It brings you
what you want hand and foot, hand and foot.

The reed is pretext. That's not its fault.
A sound of wings, nothing seen.
Pretext to what? Everything is pretext to God,
for drawing the people of God to God.

We are beggars. Everything a beggar has
was given to him by the Rich and All-Sufficient.
We're total darkness. God is light.
Sun comes in our houses and mixes with shadows.
Climb out on the roof if you want more light.
If you don't want to live depressed any longer,
move into the sun. The sun.

Who gets up early to discover the moment light begins?
Who finds us here circling, bewildered, like atoms?
Who comes to a spring thirsty
and sees the moon reflected in it?
Who, like Jacob blind with grief and age,
smells the shirt of his lost son
and can see again?
Who lets a bucket down and brings up
a flowing prophet? Or like Moses, goes for fire
and finds what burns inside the sunrise?

Jesus slips into a house to escape enemies,
and opens a door to the other world.
Solomon cuts open a fish, and there's a gold ring.
Omar storms in to kill the Prophet
and leaves with blessings.
Chase a deer and end up everywhere!
An oyster opens his mouth to swallow one drop.
Now there's a pearl.
A vagrant wanders empty ruins.
Suddenly he's wealthy.

But don't be satisfied with stories, how things
have gone with others. Unfold
your own myth, without complicated explanation,
so everyone will understand the passage,
We have opened you.

Start walking toward Shams. Your legs will get heavy
and tired. Then comes a moment
of feeling the wings you've grown,
lifting.

A baby pigeon stands on the edge of a nest all day.
Then he hears a whistle, *Come to me.*
How could he not fly toward that?
Wings tear through the body's robe
when a letter arrives
that says,
    "You've flapped and fluttered against limits
long enough.

You've been a bird without wings in a house without doors
or windows.

Compassion builds a door.
Restlessness cuts a key.

Ask. Step off into air like a baby pigeon.
Strut proudly into sunlight,
not looking back.

Take sips of this pure wine being poured.
Don't mind that you've been given a dirty cup."

I am sober now. Hand me my turban.
Fill the skin jug, or give it back empty,
whichever. A toast, Innkeeper!
Half a cup for you, half for us.
No. Wait.

Give us a full container!
You who lure men and women into this longing!
Break down my door tonight! Steal what I claim to own.
The ocean could be fresh and clear
if you would spill two drops in its water.

The moon and the evening star would dip down like birds,
if you threw the last of your wine into the air.

Daybreak comes glowing from your green vault.
You measure and pour out a beaker of twilight bloodredness.
Gliding and whirling, many miles wide,
your ocean storms come in to shore.

With all its trying and giving up,
the moon's cap falls off the back of its head
as it lifts to see you.

Every morning the birds re-word their complaining,
the songs they sing, by musicians
already with you inside the grass.

Spirit wants to see. Love wants a lover.
You set flowing four flowings through the orchard:
Pure streamwater, glowing honey,
fresh milk, dark red wine.

You don't give me a chance. Wine on top of wine,
I have no head, no way
to describe this cup.

In a sky so restless and changing
the moon wears a silver belt. Every detail,
every feature of every thing, shows how
that one is in love.

We strain and ask, then grow tired of talking.
The reed pipe crying with breath gets quiet.

As we open your door, please be there. Be held
by a gratefulness that wants you head to toe.

Inside this new love, die.
Your way begins on the other side.
Become the sky.
Take an axe to the prison wall.
Escape.
Walk out like someone suddenly born into color.
Do it now.
You're covered with thick cloud.
Slide out the side. Die,
and be quiet. Quietness is the surest sign
that you've died.
Your old life was a frantic running
from silence.

The speechless full moon
comes out now.

24

The moon has come back out,
the *other moon*, that was never above us,
or seen in dreams, the moon that brings fire
and pours wine, the host that cooks us
to tenderness.

Our eyes look at the prepared sight
and say, *Well done. Bravo!*

Then we remember the ocean
and leap out of our personalities into that.
Try to find us!

The sun goes down,
with a line of clouds running to catch up.

It's a habit of yours to walk slowly.
You hold a grudge for years.
With such heaviness, how can you be modest?
With such attachments, do you expect to arrive anywhere?

Be wide as the air to learn a secret.
Right now you're equal portions clay
and water, thick mud.

Abraham learned how the sun and moon and the stars all set.
He said, *No longer will I try to assign partners for God.*

You are so weak. Give up to Grace.
The ocean takes care of each wave
till it gets to shore.
You need more help than you know.
You're trying to live your life in open scaffolding.
Say Bismillah, *In the name of God,*
as the priest does with a knife when he offers an animal.

Bismillah your old self
to find your real name.

26

My worst habit is I get so tired of winter
I become a torture to those I'm with.

If you're not here, nothing grows.
I lack clarity. My words
tangle and knot up.

How to cure bad water? Send it back to the river.
How to cure bad habits? Send me back to you.

When water gets caught in habitual whirlpools,
dig a way out through the bottom
to the ocean. There is a secret medicine
given only to those who hurt so hard
they can't hope.

The hopers would feel slighted if they knew.

Look as long as you can at the friend you love,
no matter whether that friend is moving away from you
or coming back toward you.

Has anyone seen the boy who used to come here?
Round-faced trouble-maker, quick to find a joke, slow
to be serious. Red shirt,
perfect coordination, sly,
strong muscles, with things always in his pocket: reed flute,
ivory pick, polished and ready for his talent.
You know that one.

Have you heard stories about him?
Pharoah and the whole Egyptian world
collapsed for such a Joseph.
I'd gladly spend years getting word
of him, even third or fourth-hand.

Your face here suddenly, like Spring.
Applause, laughter. You sit
in the pomegranate branches so tickled
with the beauty. This town would disappear
without the sound of your opening,
your creeknoise-laughing, like the deep redness
of hundreds of roses.

Inside the love-forest a lion walks
looking for laughter. Dawn.
The sun comes up from a different direction!
The Lord is tricky today.
No one knows what next.

Shams and God's qualities in Shams
compose an ocean around us
where laughter-pearls plump into being.

29

Let your laughing face keep laughing.
Like a moon, not born out of anyone, but
if it had been, it would have been
born laughing!

Joseph is elevated to the judgment chambers in Egypt.
Listen to the laughter from in there!

Locked double doors blow open.
Water pours. Fire catches. Wind breaks up!
The Spring ground lifts a little finger.
It's all laughing.

Water opens the garden like a new friendship.
Leaf says to fruit, "Quit scratching your ear,
and come outside."

The sweet grape makes the deepest teacher,
because its trunk is spindly.

Lust is a winter the garden contracts in,
for how long? Too long.

Wash your face with Spring water.
Now a branch of blooms talks to the basil,
Lie down.
           Birds say to trees, *Hold us.*
A rose to God:
                Don't let winter come again.

The reply:

            "Don't grieve over December,
            or Mongol tribes that raid Khorasan.
            That is my concern.

            Juice doesn't flow from fruit,
            unless you squeeze them.
            I give unnumbered life
            when I take away the numbers.
            I serve wine that gives no headache
            when I withhold the headache wine.

            But you go on painting pictures and blackening
            pages of print, like smoke obscuring light.
            Read the day instead of books.

            Get off your horse and let him ride away,
            the perfect equestrian."

31

Spring, and no one can be still,
with all the messages coming through.

We walk outside as though going to meet visitors,
wild roses, trilliums by the water.

A tight knot loosens.
Something which died in December
lifts a head out,
and opens.

Trees, the tribe gathers!
Who has a chance
against such an elegant assemblage?

Before this power,
human beings are chives to be chopped,
gnats to be waved away.

The musician draws his hand across the strings,
so the idlers will come in off the street.
Those who have been waiting start to work.
The thieves of inner qualities no longer threaten.
They're brought to justice.
The figurers can't read their own columns of figures.
Friend calls friend to a secret cave.

Saddle the nimble horses with gold-inlaid leather.
Let the pack-horses continue with their loads.
Comfort the grieving, not those who think only
of how to sell things. The sensualities they live for
are sharp points pushing into their flesh.
Those who walk into fire feel refreshed,
who run to water scald themselves.

The dusty face of Moses moves toward light.
Pharoah parades into stupidity and humiliation.
The mystery of the way is the old trick
of reversing horseshoes. Moses bends
to pick up a stick. It's alive.

33

Spring, and everything outside is growing, even the tall cypress tree.
We must not leave this place.
Around the lip of the cup we share, these words:

My Life Is Not Mine

If someone were to play music, it would have to be very sweet.
We're drinking wine, but not through lips.
We're sleeping it off, but not in bed.
Rub the cup across your forehead.
This day is outside living and dying.

Give up wanting what other people have.
That way you're safe.
"Where, where can I be safe?" you ask.

This is not a day for asking questions,
not a day on any calendar.
This day is conscious of itself.
This day is a lover, bread and gentleness,
more manifest than saying can say.

Thoughts take form with words,
but this daylight is beyond and before
thinking and imagining. Those two,
they are so thirsty, but this gives smoothness
to water. Their mouths are dry, and they are tired.

The rest of this poem is too blurry
for them to read.

It's lucky to hear the flutes for dancing
coming down the road. The ground is glowing.
The table set in the yard.

We will drink all this wine tonight
because it's Spring. It is.
It's a growing sea. We're clouds
over the sea,
or flecks of matter
in the ocean when the ocean seems lit from within.
I know I'm drunk when I start this ocean talk.

Would you like to see the moon split
in half with one throw?

I've heard that a certain man lost his camel.
He goes everywhere, not finding that camel.
He falls asleep in the desert by the side of the road,
tired and thinking now he's through looking.

Late in the night he wakes up full of that loss.
The moon comes rolling out like a white ball
on the huge, empty polo field of the sky.
By that light he sees his camel standing
in the middle of the road. His tears
come easily like a quick rain.

He turns his face up, wet and shining.
How can I say what you are with your light?

Let this be a night like that one.
Each second the moon tells us, *Be more passionate.*
We should shine back and tell it the same thing.

It makes us restless. It grieves for us.
Take it inside you, that One whose Presence
is water. We are the stream, searching along.
That One is musk. We are the way musk smells.
Why not spray ourselves?

When I see you and how you are,
I close my eyes to the other.
For your Solomon's seal I become wax
throughout my body. I wait to be light.
I give up opinions on all matters.
I become the reed flute for your breath.

You were inside my hand.
I kept reaching around for something.
I was inside your hand, but I kept asking questions
of those who know very little.

I must have been incredibly simple or drunk or insane
to sneak into my own house and steal money,
to climb over the fence and take my own vegetables.
But no more. I've gotten free of that ignorant fist
that was pinching and twisting my secret self.

The universe and the light of the stars come through me.
I am the crescent moon put up
over the gate to the festival.

Every day is Friday,
the beginning of holidays, holy days.

Isn't last Friday remembered now with a festival?
You have on the right clothes for this festival,
your light, your clear trusting,
your inside and outside the same,
not a sweet walnut filled with garlic.

Go around in this ring
like a lover on the doorstep of a lover.
How can straw be still on a river?
How can a mystic stay angry?

To some eyes these words are a new-green branch.
To sensual eyes, they are old matters
carved on a building.

Someone says, *Sanai is dead.*
No small thing to say.

He was not bits of husk,
or a puddle that freezes overnight,
or a comb that cracks when you use it,
or a pod crushed open on the ground.

He was fine powder in a rough clay dish.
He knew what both worlds were worth:
A grain of barley.

One he slung down, the other up.

The inner soul, that presence of which most know nothing,
about which poets are so ambiguous,
he married that one to the Beloved.

His pure gold wine pours on the thick wine-dregs.
They mix and rise and separate again
to meet down the road. Dear Friend from Marghaz,
who lived in Rayy, in Rum, Kurd from the mountains,
each of us returns home.

Silk must not be compared with striped canvas.

Be quiet and clear now
like the final touchpoints of calligraphy.

Your name has been erased
from the roaring volume of speech.

39

You bind me, and I tear away in a rage to open out
into air, a round brightness, a candlepoint,
all reason, all love.

This confusing joy, your doing,
this hangover, your tender thorn.

You turn to look, I turn.
I'm not saying this right.

I am a jailed crazy who ties up spirit-women.
I am Solomon.

What goes comes back. Come back.
We never left each other.

A disbeliever hides disbelief,
but I will say his secret.

More and more awake, getting up at night,
spinning and falling with love for Shams.

40

I tried to think of some way
to let my face become his.

"Could I whisper in your ear
a dream I've had? You're the only one
I've told this to."

He tilts his head, laughing,
as if, "I know the trick you're hatching,
but go ahead."

I am an image he stitches with gold thread
on a tapestry, the least figure,
a playful addition.

But nothing he works on is dull.
I am part of the beauty.